LAILA WHITAKER

Smart Money Management

A Simple Savings Strategy for Financial Success

First edition

This book was professionally typeset on Reedsy.
Find out more at reedsy.com

Contents

1

Introduction

I am very lucky that my father taught my brother and me the importance of saving and gifting money from a very young age. Back in the mid to late 1960s my brother and I would each receive an allowance of 25 cents every Friday for doing chores and helping around the house. We were probably around five or six years old. Per my father's instructions, ten percent went to our savings accounts, and ten percent went to charity. The rest we could spend however we wished. As time went on, our allowance grew to one dollar a week. Later, there were babysitting and other odd jobs. You would be surprised at how much your savings (even ten cents a week) grows even though the weekly amount seems so meager. Especially today.

Unfortunately, as the years have passed I have noticed that so many people live paycheck to paycheck and spend a lot of money for instant gratification and non-essential items rather than planning for their futures. They often live *at* or *above* their means. What do I mean by that? Your means is your income from paychecks and any other money you might receive including gifts, winnings or bonuses. Month to month, there is no budget or plan; so all of the money is spent almost immediately each time they have money in their hands. Many spend more money than they have via credit cards, as well. Now there is debt to contend with. Sound familiar? They are living at or above their means. If there is an emergency or unexpected expense, there is no money left for that. Again, their debt grows.

This simple guide is a result of what I was taught as a child along with some revisions that I have discovered along the way. This strategy is meant to be a basic plan for you to be successful with your money regardless of your age. If you stick with the plan and make it a habit, a rule for yourself, you will be pleased with the long-term results.

Your mission is to be able to live below your means comfortably so that you can accomplish what it is you would like to achieve without stress. If you want a simple plan without having to sit down and make a formal "budget," perhaps forgetting things to add or making it more complicated than it has to be, getting flustered because it appears that you're not earning enough income, or you just do not know where to start, then this guide is for you.

2

The Strategy

Have you heard the old proverb, "A fool and his money are soon parted?" If you do not really have a plan or budget, then you are flying by the seat of your pants. You do not really have command of what money you have available for your expenses and no plan for saving any money. The strategy here is to make a plan for all of your income so that you can be prepared for what life throws at you. What will life throw at you besides your basic monthly expenses? Marriage, babies, medical bills, education expenses, loss of a job, retirement, etc. Who knows? The possibilities are endless. Money doesn't grow on trees, you know.

So, let's get started.

Each of the following chapters is dedicated to accounts that you will set up for your success.

3

Checking Account

I have heard several experts say to pay yourself first. Well, okay. We'll start there. If you do not already have one, you will need to open a checking account from which you will pay all of your monthly bills. Find a checking account that will pay you some interest. Sixty percent of all of your income will be deposited into your checking account. By income, I mean all of the money you take home (after taxes) from your job, gifts, winnings, or bonuses.

For the purpose of this account, your monthly expenses include all of the necessities that you need in order to live. You might have noticed that I used the word "necessities." This does not include non-essential items such as lottery tickets, eating out, entertainment, etc. Are your monthly expenses greater than 60% of your monthly income? Then you had better find ways to either increase your income or lower your expenses or both.

Do you need to increase your income? You could start your own side hustle. Have a garage sale or sell unwanted items or items that you do not need online. Rent out a room in your home (more on that later).

Perhaps you can get a second job or part-time work temporarily until you're comfortable with your money management progress.

Do you need to lower your expenses? Get creative. It is advantageous to shop around regularly for your automobile insurance and your home or rental insurance. Try shopping for needed clothing at the local thrift store or at discount retailers. Use the coupons that arrive in your mailbox each week. Shop the sales at the grocery store. Only buy what you need at the grocery store. Why don't you walk or ride a bike if you are not going far. Make sure that you are not using a credit card that charges a yearly fee. Use the grill outside instead of your oven or stove during the hot summer months. Turn off the lights when you leave the room. Conserve your water usage. Look at each of your monthly expenses and think of ways to lower them. All of these things add up. This checking account is for your living expenses, such as:

Rent or Mortgage

This is probably your biggest expense if you are paying rent or if you have a mortgage. This is your top priority each month because you want to keep a roof over your head. Pay this first. If you are renting or a homeowner, can you lower this expense by getting a roommate? Whether you are renting or not, would you consider renting out a room in your home on a short-term basis? There are several online venues for advertising short-term vacation rentals. If you are renting, this might be allowed in your contract. Speak with your landlord. Whether you are a renter or a homeowner, research your local laws and restrictions.

Automobile and Transportation

This might be your next largest expense. Are you making car payments?

Often, buying a used car and paying for repairs along the way is less expensive than paying monthly car payments for a new car. Do you know of a mechanic you can trust? Ask the expert to check out the car before you buy it.

Do you live in a larger city where you are paying for parking or transportation? It can be a lot less expensive to fully utilize public transportation rather than making monthly car payments and worrying about repairs and buying gas. If you are paying for a parking garage while you are at work, shop around. Find out where your co-workers are parking. You might find a better deal.

Utilities

This includes your phone bill, electricity, television streaming, cable, internet, water, and gas. This is definitely an area of your expenses over which you actually have some control. Think about all the electronic devices you currently have plugged into your walls right now. Even if it is on standby, like your coffee pot, it is using some electricity. What temperature is your thermostat set to? Can it be adjusted? What is the thermostat set to when you are working away from home? Also, call your electric company. Many offer free home energy checks. There are also several online videos to help you find and fix air leaks in your home. These things might sound like pennies per month, but all of those pennies certainly add up quickly.

Conserve your water. Turn off the faucet while you are brushing your teeth. Turn it back on to clean your toothbrush and rinse. The next time you take a shower, time yourself. Are you wasting any time? These are habits you are capable of changing. Do you have any leaking faucets inside or outside? There are also online videos to help with that.

Do you have a landline and a cell phone? Chances are, you do not need both. Get rid of one of them. What will be the most cost effective for you, cable or streaming? Do you need all the streaming channels you are paying for? Do you need all the cable channels you are paying for? Call your internet provider to find out if you are paying for more than what you really need. If you are not into serious gaming, you might not need the super fast speeds your Internet provider offers.

Food

Generally, food is much cheaper to buy at the grocery store rather than eating out. When you need something on the go, grocery stores have lots of options. You do not like cooking? You do not have time to cook? Grocery stores have hot, cooked food options, bagged salads, pre-cut fruits and vegetables, deli items, frozen foods, heat and eat items, etc. Many grocery stores are even offering delivery to your door. That is even more convenient than driving to a fast-food joint or other restaurant.

Clothing

Go through all of your clothing piece by piece. Sell or donate anything that you have not worn in a year. If you are not ready to do that, flip all of the hangers in your closet backwards. As you wear and wash your clothes, hang them in your closet normally. In a year's time, you will see what you have not worn for the last 12 months. Sell, hand down, or donate the clothing still hanging on the flipped hangers. If there are items you need, try the thrift stores. This not only saves you money and gives you the opportunity for unique finds, but you are saving items from ending up in a landfill somewhere.

Credit cards

Pay them off each month. You do not want to pay the credit card company any interest if you do not have to. Why would you want to pay more for the items you already have? If you cannot pay the entire amount, pay as much as possible so that you can get to the position in a few months of being able to pay the entire monthly amount. Try not to use more than one credit card. There is less to keep track of that way.

Remember, with your new plan, this checking account is for paying for essential items listed in this chapter. If you are purchasing non-essential items or making donations, etc., with your credit card, you may want to reimburse your checking account from your other savings accounts. Alternatively, you can pay those portions of your bill directly from your other accounts. Do what works best for you as long as you are sticking to your plan.

Insurance

This includes your vehicle, home, rental, medical, and any other insurance you might have. This is another area you should research yearly. Shop around. These companies are competing for your business and often advertise that they can save you money by switching to them. Do your homework, annually, at least. Some companies offer incentives for staying with them. Regardless, shop around and make sure that they continue to be your best option.

Miscellaneous

Medications, personal hygiene items, cleaning supplies, etc., are more examples of the items you will be purchasing with this checking account. Get creative with how you can lower your expenses in these areas without hurting yourself or making yourself miserable. Continue to take your prescribed medications. Make sure you are keeping yourself and your surroundings clean. Stay healthy and happy!

If you already have pets, I would never suggest that you give them away. Pets are a part of your family. However, if you are struggling to pay your monthly bills and thinking about it, do not get a new pet. This should be common sense. They are expensive. In addition to the rest of your expenses, you will have to buy, at the very least, pet food. There are vet bills. Just as in humans, you never know when your pet might get ill and require a veterinarian's services.

Eventually, you will be able to keep a "cushion" of income in your checking account. You will not spend everything in your account each month. Each month will vary. Often, as people gain more income, they tend to spend more. Try not to do that as you continue to grow your accounts. This is living *below* your means.

4

Savings Account

While you are opening your checking account, open a savings account, as well. Many banks will connect the two accounts so that if you happen to overspend on your checking account, it is automatically deducted from your savings account without penalties. However, it is best if you keep an eye on your money to make sure that does not happen. It defeats the real purpose of your savings account. Also, research several banks. What each bank offers in terms of interest payments and minimum balances varies widely.

Deposit 10% of all of your after tax income into this savings account. This account is for all of your unexpected necessary expenses. Additionally, it can also be used for specific items you need to purchase.

You will notice that these examples all fall into the category of essential items. Now and then, there will be unexpected events that will require an outlay of cash. It is best to be ready. Of course, if you can cover these expenses with your checking account money, you are ahead of the game! Examples of what you might use the money from this account are:

Home Repairs and Auto Repairs

If you own a home, then you know that it seems like there is always something that needs fixing or replacing. Appliances, air conditioners, water heaters, garage door openers, etc., all eventually stop working. This can be catastrophic for those who have not planned for these events in advance. This account can also be used to save for home improvements such as a new roof, painting, and updating. Just be sure to save funds for the improvements in this account before you make the purchase. Paying credit card interest defeats the purpose of trying to save. Do your preventative maintenance. Change the filters, clean your air conditioning unit, change the batteries in your smoke alarm, and so on.

The same goes for your automobile. Keep your vehicle in good condition with regular oil changes and maintenance. This will save you money in repairs in the long run. Have you run your car into the ground, and you are ready for a different vehicle? Consider buying a used car with low mileage. Shop around. When you find the car you wish to buy, you might want to let your mechanic check it out for you.

Medical Emergencies

My kidney cancer surgery and my husband's quadruple bypass surgery, both in the last five years, were definitely not planned. Those surgeries were sudden, terrible surprises. Fortunately, we each had medical insurance to take care of most of the expenses. However, there were deductibles and follow-up doctor's visits, which also came into play. For us, money was not an issue because we have this planned savings account in place. I do not wish any unfortunate events on others, but I do urge you to decide to put this plan in place for yourself. Just in case of such an emergency.

Vacations and Trips

I encourage you to plan yearly vacations and trips. They are a nice distraction from the hustle and bustle of everyday life. You need a recharge at least once a year. These do not have to be expensive. They can be excursions near your home to eliminate hotel or camping costs. There are many city, state and federal parks in every state that offer excellent hiking, swimming, fishing, and other activities. Save and plan for a visit to a nearby amusement park. Check out museums, some of which have free days. Go to a professional ball game. Visit a botanical garden. Spend a day driving and sight-seeing. Check out the roadside attractions when one catches your eye. Make a friend or relative's place your home base, and explore their neck of the woods.

For some, it is easier to make a separate account for vacations. If this works for you, go for it. We have a very large "change jar" that we keep in our bedroom. We put some money in it daily. Even if it is just a penny we found on the ground in a parking lot. When it fills up, we relax and enjoy rolling all the change into coin wrappers and taking them to the bank together. We are always surprised at how much money we have saved. Check with your bank's policies. Some banks charge for accepting coins and some do not. Some banks even provide the coin wrappers!

Education

Perhaps you are saving money for your education or your children's education. Again, you might want to make this a separate account to which you add 10% of your income each time you receive income. Otherwise, if your education includes seminars, books, or other programs that you purchase on your own, this is the account for that purpose. I encourage you to do something each month to educate yourself, whether it be podcasts, online videos, books, or a visit to a historical place or museum. You will not be sorry.

Miscellaneous

There are a few annual expenses that you might incur, like property taxes and income taxes. This is the appropriate account for planning for those expenses, as well.

Perhaps you need new furniture. Consider estate sales, second-hand stores, thrift shops, and flea markets. Sometimes you can find exactly what you are looking for where you least expect it.

Big events can also be big expenses. Are you planning to get engaged and get married? Are you throwing a graduation or anniversary party or other holiday party? These things do not have to be really expensive. Get creative. Get ideas from friends and relatives. I am sure you can think of a lot of stuff that you might want to be saving for. Decide what your priorities are and save accordingly.

5

Investment Account

I recommend opening another savings account for this step. It does not have to be at the same bank as your initial checking and savings accounts. Again, do your research to get the best interest rates and minimum balance thresholds. It is important to get some of your money to work for you. Deposit 10% of your income into this account.

You might not want to use these funds immediately. Let this account grow. This gives you some time to educate yourself for when you think you might be interested in making an investment into something. If you are investing in someone else's business, seriously consider hiring an attorney to make sure your agreement is in order, legal, and in writing.

Of course, your age and the objectives in your life will determine the types of items you will want to invest in. If you are already retired, purchasing a long-term investment might not be an attractive option unless you plan to flip it fairly quickly. Some examples of where you can invest your money as you build this account are as follows:

Purchase Land or Property

I have had mostly good experiences over the years investing in land, homes and rental properties. Historically, it has been considered a safe investment. Know what you are getting into. Is your property governed by an HOA? Is it in a flood zone? What will the yearly property taxes cost? Is it a safe neighborhood? What type of growth is happening in the area?

If you are getting into the business of rental property, study your local and federal laws. Seriously think about how much work that entails. Will this be a short-term rental property? Should you hire a property manager? Will you be mowing the lawn there or hiring it out? What will the renter be responsible for? What are your responsibilities as the landlord? What sort of paperwork do I need to keep for tax purposes? What are your risks? Will you need special insurance? Again, do your research and keep your eyes open for good opportunities.

Invest in Stocks and Bonds

By all means, if you work at a company offering to match what you contribute to a 401K account or something similar, sign up right away. This is pay above your regular wages. Free money.

Additionally, you may want to invest in your own IRA account in which you or a professional financial agent buys and sells stocks and bonds in the market. This is an area that can be volatile. There are even names for the volatility: bear and bull markets. A bear market is when prices are trending downward. A bull market is the opposite as the prices are trending upward. As it is with most investments, do your homework. There are books written about choosing stocks and playing the market. There are financial professionals who you can hire to choose stocks for you or to help you make educated buying and selling decisions. In fact, they can look over your entire portfolio of accounts, assets and investments and give you suggestions and pointers.

Start Your Own Business or Side Hustle

There are many people with more than one job. Your own side hustle or business that you own can be a part-time or full-time endeavor. What are you interested in? What do you enjoy doing? Do you have a talent, like playing an instrument or entertaining in some other way? Are you an avid gardener? Are you a great cook? Do you love helping people organize? Are you great at throwing parties? These are all skills that people might be willing to pay someone to do for them. As always, do your homework. Is a license required? Is a certain level of education expected? Check the local laws.

Invest in Someone Else's Business or Idea

Perhaps you have saved the money, but you do not feel that you have the time. Why not invest in someone else's idea or business. How do you find these people? Just keep your ears open. Notice when someone you are speaking with or overhearing mentions an idea that sounds appealing to you. Of course, do your homework and ask the right questions. What will be expected of you? Have an attorney draw up the necessary papers for your agreement in this investment.

6

Gifting Account

I suggest that for this account, you do not open another savings account unless you have thousands of dollars that you are saving for a specific charity or charity event. Instead, I would keep this money in a separate place at home. Ideally, keep money for donations in a large labeled envelope that is easy for you to get to. This way, you have cash on hand when the girl scouts arrive at your door with delicious cookies, or the boy scouts arrive at your door with tasty popcorn.

This one is pretty self explanatory. However, you might be wondering why you would save money for gifting when you are really trying to save money for yourself. Many people make donations in the name of their religious convictions, spirituality, Karma, universal law, or cause and effect. Do good things, and good things will come to you. Make room for planned gifting, and gifts will come to you. Does it happen immediately? Sometimes. Besides, it feels good to help people.

Place a sheet of paper in the envelope along with the money you will be gifting, as well as receipts, to keep track of your donations for tax purposes. You might even just keep track of your gifting habits for your own awareness. Additionally, you might want to keep a small envelope (marked donations) with gifting money in your purse, wallet, or pocket, especially during the holidays, for making donations or helping the homeless if you are so inclined. Here are some suggestions of uses for this account:

Places of Worship and Spirituality

There are countless places of worship and spirituality, most of which are not-for-profit organizations. A collection plate is often passed around, and attendees will want to contribute. Now that you have an account for this purpose, you know immediately the amount you have saved to offer.

Charitable Contributions and Charity Events

You may have a pet charitable organization that you feel strongly about supporting. You might belong to a club or organization that holds events for specific charities. Especially near the holidays, it seems that we see a lot of donation opportunities and charitable events in which we would enjoy participating.

If you are not interested in any particular charitable organization, do some research on the Internet. Find an area that interests you. Donating to special causes helps others, and that makes us feel good.

Scholarships and School Supplies

After learning that a certain celebrity donates three scholarships each year at my alma mater, Ball State University, I have always wanted to present a small scholarship to a person at my old high school who will be furthering their education and graduates at the same rank that I did, around #33 out of over 500 students. It has not happened yet, but it will. As you can see, you can get inspiration for recipients of your donations from friends, a need that you discover, news stories, celebrities, athletes and more.

At the beginning of each school year, I hear of teachers who are paying for their students' school supplies out of their own pockets. Maybe this is coming from their own gifting accounts, but I would bet they would welcome some help from others, as well.

Gifts for Friends and Family

Perhaps you are more inclined to give gifts to people you are more familiar with or the people you know. Maybe you do not have to look very far to find that those close to you also could use some help. This could include local families in need, those whose house burned down or became flooded. If they are not willing to accept a gift, you can get creative. Bring food, take them out for lunch, give them rides to appointments, take them to a movie, etc.

You might hear of someone else doing nice things for people in your community. Why not join them? There is an uplifting ripple effect. Have you ever heard of the pay-it-forward movement? Essentially, you do something nice for someone. Instead of getting paid back, your recipient does something nice for someone else, and so on. The funding for these acts of kindness can come from this account.

7

Blow-it Account

Again, I would not open an account for money that I am just going to spend soon. I would keep this in an envelope or, better yet, a pretty container with a lid. Do not carry it around with you. It will be too tempting to spend it on the fly without really thinking about how you would like to reward yourself. This is the account from which we can give ourselves gifts. It gives us another thing to look forward to. It can be something extravagant or just something you want.

Think of this account as your short-term reward for sticking with your money management program. Your other accounts will be rewarding in the long run, but you need a way to celebrate right away! Give yourself permission to spend every cent in your blow-it account every month or every other month if you want to. Do what keeps you motivated and happy. I am guessing that you really do not need any help with ideas, but here are some examples of what a blow-it account can be used for to get your creative juices flowing:

· Extravagant items

- Date night
- Outings
- A cruise
- Movies
- Dinner out
- Wagyu steak
- Jewelry
- Nice bottle of wine
- Massages
- Concert tickets
- A night at the casino
- Buy lottery tickets
- A helicopter ride around the city
- Anything that is not a necessity

.

8

Conclusion

Regardless of your age or your current income, the important thing to remember is to make your plan and to stick with it. Trust that the money will grow. My suggestions can easily be adjusted for your own special circumstances. Do you need more funding for education, a wedding or vacations? Maybe you have a child on the way. Then it might be advantageous for you to open a separate account for those savings. Maybe it's easier for you to keep some money in a jar for your blow-it account or vacations. Do what works for you. You can always make changes along the way.

Start with the program outlined in this book, and then you may make adjustments as you go. Maybe you have the means to deposit more than 10% into your investments account and less in your regular checking account. That's great! Just be sure that you continue to save something from each paycheck in all these areas. I hope that this short synopsis inspires you to begin your money management plan. I hope that this plan will be as helpful to you as it has been in my life. I hope that you are eager to start your money management plan. You will watch your net worth grow instead of struggling to make ends meet. It's never too early to begin, and it is not too late, either. You will wonder why you haven't done something like this sooner. Simply set yourself (and your children) up for financial success!

- 60% Checking Account
- 10% Savings Account
- 10% Investment Account
- 10% Gifting Account
- 10% Blow-it Account

I hope you enjoyed this book, which is filled with the simple monetary advice that I wholeheartedly believe in, because it has worked for me. If you enjoyed Smart Money Management, I would love to read your positive feedback in the review section on Amazon.com. Even just a short one or two sentence review would be greatly appreciated. Your feedback is valuable to me so that I can produce more high quality content. Thank you so much for purchasing this book!

CONCLUSION

9

Resources

A bout *David Letterman. (n.d.). https://www.bsu.edu/web/letterman/about#:~:text=Campus%20radio%20station%20WCRD%20began,%2410%2C000%2C%20%245%2C000%2C%20and%20%243%2C333.*

Airbnb your place. (n.d.). Airbnb. https://www.airbnb.com/host/homes

Chang, E., & Cybulski, A. (2023, April 13). Where can you exchange coins for cash? *US News & World Report.* https://www.usnews.com/banking/articles/want-to-cash-in-your-coins-your-bank-may-be-the-best-place#:~:text=Yes%2C%20You%20Can%20Deposit%20Coins,Check%20your%20bank's%20policy.

Eker, T. H. (2005). *Secrets of the Millionaire Mind: Mastering the inner game of wealth.* http://ci.nii.ac.jp/ncid/BB02345285

Evans, R. P. (2006b). *Five lessons a millionaire taught me about life and wealth.* Simon & Schuster Audio.

Folger, J. (2021). The truth about real estate prices. *Investopedia.* https://www.investopedia.com/articles/mortages-real-estate/11/the-truth-about-the-realestatemarket.asp#:~:text=Home%20values%20tend%20to%20rise,other%20areas%20struggle%20to%20rebound.

Kiyosaki, R. T. (2000). *Rich Dad Poor Dad - What the Rich Teach Their Kids About Money* (Abridged edition) [Book]. Business Plus.